Echoes of My Life

Susan Jeavons

Presentation by *BookLeaf Publishing*

Web: www.bookleafpub.com

E-mail: info@bookleafpub.com

ISBN: 9789357442022

First edition 2023

DEDICATION

I dedicate this book to my daughters and my late son, with love.

ACKNOWLEDGEMENT

I'd like to thank my children for encouraging me to keep writing. Also a dear friend name Cristi who sent me the link to this site.

PREFACE

My father was a pedophile. Poetry was my escape, my panacea. My hope is that other survivors will read my book and find the courage to tell their stories. I am at peace with my past and have forgiven my abusers. They have both passed on.

Perpetual Cleansing

It is time once more
to scrub every exposed pore,
every wretched, weeping wound.

Steam rises like a magical potion,
surrounds me like a sanitizing rain
that purifies all that was stained.

Salty tears trickle upon tiled floor,
fuse with fetid pieces of the past
until my soul is clean once more.

Tomorrow, when truth of incest settles in
I will begin the ritual
all over again…

A Mother's Love

Take away the treasures,
the photos and the lace,
take away the teddy bears
that decorate the place,
now close your eyes and picture
the memories tucked away,
of laughter and of music
that echoed here each day.

Take away the children
who danced across this floor.
Take away the fingerprints
that kissed each wall and door.
Now close your eyes and picture
a young girl sitting there
rocking a tiny baby
with lullaby and prayer.

Take away the struggles,
the tears that she has cried.
Take away her hopes and dreams
then take away her pride.
Now close your eyes and tell me
what is it that you see?
The spirit of a mothers love
that lasts eternally.

Hope Lives

In the eyes of the abused
women and children, dejected, used,
survivors determined to succeed
concealing wounds that never bleed.

In the hearts of widows and lonely souls
eager for love to make them whole,
in crowded asylums, foster care
abandoned children everywhere,
hope lives.

It's evident in daughters and sons
who escaped death by lethal guns
then testify how they forgive
and pray for those who did not live,

In cardboard shacks whole families stay,
in rusty cars they live and pray.
Hope has no face, not rich or poor,
but lives in peace, and lives in war.

Our spirits thrive on this belief
it fills our emptiness, soothes our grief.
We trust in better things to come
with the promise of tomorrow
at least for some,
hope lives...

Musical Lobotomy

If I could purge
that part of my brain
which stores pain,

I would replace it
with a gentle refrain;
Bach, Beethoven

or simply rain…

Incomplete Metamorphosis

There are days,
when I want to forget,
wipe the slate clean,
become someone new.

There are days when
apple pies and lilac skies
can slightly modify,
yet inside

I am seven
afraid
      alone
            betrayed...

The Offering

Here Daddy-
take her.
Isn't she pretty?
She looks
a lot like me.
You can
hold her
and squeeze her
and touch her
and she won't cry
or bleed
or tell,

I promise...

I Am the Child

You and I have never met
But I am the child you must not forget.
I am the child who whimpered in pain.
I am the child who was beaten and slain.
I am the child who cried at night.
I am the child whose future was bright.
I am the child whose fear was real.
I am the child whose scars won't heal.
I am the child you see each day,
Who is not your problem, so you turn away.
I am the child, the child so small
Who only wanted to be loved, that's all.
You and I have never met,
But I am the child you must not forget.

Fog Monster

The fog moved in,
stretched far and wide,
consuming everything outside.
It traveled the mountains,
valleys and seas,
devouring buildings, ships and trees.

Like a burglar in the night,
the fog snatched everything in sight,
and left no trace with light of day,
turned his back and crawled away.

I Invited A Dragon To Dinner

That was almost the wrong thing to do!
Have you ever seen what a dragon
can do to a bowl of beef stew?
The carrots were shrunken and shriveled!
The celery-quite a sad sight,
yet the dragon seemed rather delighted
as he gobbled up every last bite!
The salad was quite a disaster
with the croutons burnt to a crisp
and the lettuce was beyond recognition
and wilted into a green wisp!
Still, that dragon ate every last morsel
and was pleased as a dragon could be!
cause he roared and burped rather loudly,
but politely exclaimed, "Pardon me!"
Next I passed the desert to the dragon
as we giggled and talked for a spell.
Then the dragon thanked me profusely
and uttered a steamy farewell.
He taught me to laugh at my worries,
enjoy life with good company,
so tomorrow he's coming for breakfast
and frying the bacon for me!

Harried Housewife List

Feed the puppy. Bake a cake.
Take the trash out for Heaven's sake!
Call my mother! Take a pill!
Read the paper. Write Aunt Jill.

Dentist tomorrow-be there by eight!
Pick the kids up-don't be late!
Make a salad. Bake the bread.
Feed the gerbil-OOPS! He's dead!

Puppy piddled! Burned the cake!
Take the trash out for Heaven's sake!
Mother's coming! Take some drugs!
Search the want ads! Hire some thugs!

"Hello Dear, what's that smell?
Cake or gerbil, I can't tell!
Funeral Friday for Aunt Jill."
Save that stamp and find her will!

If there's something that I missed;
put it on tomorrow's list!
Write it down and double check!
Bury that gerbil! Smells like heck!

Survival of The Fittest

Even a tree
must struggle to survive,
tossed and torn
in the wind and rain,
yet it grows stronger
and begins to thrive,
becoming greener
for all its pain.

In His Hands

When we feel like we are at the end of our rope,
when we don't see the light and we give up hope,
it's then that the Lord reaches down lifts us high,
and gives us the strength to help us get by.
With faith in our hearts and God's love we know,
all things are possible, for he told us so.

It's A Secret, I Won't Tell!

Miss McCorkle's famous meatloaf
is by far the best, a sweetloaf,
but she say's she'll never tell
how she makes it taste so swell.

I have bribed her with some flowers,
sat and begged and begged for hours,
but she's stubborn as a mule.
Never give it up's her rule!

I have tried to analyze it,
stirred it up, reorganized it,
but I can not figure out
what the secret is about.

I refuse to stop my quest.
It's too scrumptious! It's the best!
I will figure out the reason
why her meatloaf is so pleasing!

Now I think I finally know
why we love her meatloaf so.
Keep this secret! Be discreet-
that yummy loaf contains no meat!

Not a smidgen, not a speck,
not a morsel, not a fleck
of McCorkle's tasty treat
has a trace of any meat!

Hide-and-seek Child

Where did my little boy go,
the cheerful one I use to know
who'd run and play without a care?
I cannot find him anywhere.

I thought I saw him yesterday
when I looked out across the way,
a little boy beside the tree
playing hide-and-seek with me.

He disappeared without a trace
but I still see his smiling face
and feel his hand as he touched me
once upon a memory.

I blinked and he became a man.
It was not something I had planned,
but children grow so quick it seems
as if they're only ours in dreams

Becoming The River

If I were a river
nothing could hold me back,
not mountains or valleys,
not concrete or steel.
If I were a river
others would feel my power
hour after hour,
as I hurried off the beaten track
with my liquid pulse
pounding the shore,
my voice, a steady roar.
On and on without pity,
through the countryside.
around the city,
down the mountain
in a daring leap,
on and on I'd swiftly keep moving.
Churning, turning from dusk till dawn,
in sunlight or moonlight
on and on till the end of time.
Nothing would stop me
for I'm the river
and I will go on
and on
and on…

River Haiku

Here at the river
I am a child again,
full of wonder and awe…

I Am, I Am The Music!

For so long Lord I've listened
to the whispers that you send,
but I never heard their pureness,
never knew their awesome blend.
Until just now, as I listened
and I conceived with humility,
that your whispers and my talent
merge in two part harmony.

These Eyes...

I have seen eyes like this before,
eyes that have cried too many tears,
eyes that hide too many fears,
eyes that hold too much hate,
eyes that seem to always wait.
These eyes, these eyes, these brilliant eyes,
eyes that haunt and mesmerize,
eyes that mirror the soul of civilization,
eyes without hope, eyes of desperation,
eyes that look like yours and mine.
They're the eyes of the world, eyes of the divine.
These eyes, these eyes, these brilliant eyes,
tell no secrets, tell no lies.
In the mirror, there I see
the eyes, the eyes of humanity....

River Findings

The Ohio winds around hills
and streams down the hollows,
passes steel mills, brick yards
and scrap yards. It carries tug boats,
pushes barges, and hauls black coal
stripped from the mountainsides.

The Ohio's littered banks
are home to train yards
filled with graffiti-covered
box cars, rusting relics
of the Southern Pacific
and the Norfolk and Southern railroads.

Erector set bridges
span the murky river
and link Ohio
to "Wild, Wonderful, West Virginia,"
the Weirton Mill,
and Homer Laughlin China Company.

In towns called Powhaton Point,
Shadyside, Bellaire,
and East Liverpool,
houses are stacked on hillsides
with an array of slate, tin
and asbestos shingled roofs.

Ball fields and corn fields,
concrete parking lots
and shopping malls
are full of busy people
who fail to appreciate
the river's charity.

There are roads with cryptic names
like Goose Run, Pinch Run,
Riddles Run, and Rush Run.
There are towns named Brilliant,
Costonia and Calcutta, each
with their own secrets.

North on Route 7
bars advertise Karaoke
and all you can eat fish fries.
A plethora of car lots and gift shops,
bait stores and gun supplies
dot the countryside with

a never-ending display
of marketing profanity,
but the river rolls on
never compromising
her dignity,
never surrendering her boundaries.

White-steepled churches
stand like beacons of redemption,
while billboards promote
"Hellfire Fireworks,"
"Gentlemen's" clubs, sleazy motels
and the "Forbidden Zone Exit."

Still the river moves along,
proud and powerful,
chanting and rippling
with satisfaction,
a stalwart testament
to her tenacity…

Katrina's Wrath

'Twas an ill wind blowing on that August day.
'Twas a portent of what was headed that way.
All saints and sinners, aye ye better take heed,
of the storm they called Katrina.

All the anchors were down and the sails were
moored,
every shutter was nailed, every treasure was stored.
The warning went out, but some would n'er concede
to the storm they called Katrina.

Through the dark of night you could hear her roar
and the water kept rising past the reservoir,
as every saint and sinner prayed for relief
from the storm they called Katrina.

The blues never abandoned New Orleans.
By the light of day you could hear the screams,
and each day brought new devastation and grief
from the storm they called Katrina.

Days went by and no one came to the aid
of the helpless souls who were so afraid.
Still, some looted and raped and paid no heed
to the storm they called Katrina.

The swells have fallen but there still remains
the toxic sludge, and the shameful stains
on those who turned their backs that day
on the victims of Katrina.

'Twas an ill wind blowing on that August day.
'Twas a portent of the dame headed that way.
All saints and sinners, aye ye should have taken heed,
of the storm they called Katrina

of the storm they called Katrina...

Ode To the Wind

I love to watch you wind, as you sway the trees
and blow
across the fields in a gentle breeze, but I wonder
where you go.
You disappear sometimes, in a mischievous sort of
way
then when I least expect it, you come back out to
play.
You sing a tune in Winter that seems so harsh to
some,
but I for one feel lucky when I hear your music
come.
In Spring you gently billow and bring life back
again.
No matter what the season, I love to hear your
wind.
When you come a calling on a warm day in July
you fill my heart with calmness with your sweet,
sweet lullaby.
Your summer breaths are subtle with every chord
you sound,
and in Autumn you're pure magic when leaves
start rustling round.
Your icy winds of November that rouse the calmest
sea

bring danger to the sailors, but never frighten me.
For I crave to hear you murmur with bravado of
your tales
of your journey across the horizon as November's
fiercest gales.
Oh wind, Oh wind I love thee. You're music to my
ears,.
and you've given me much pleasure for oh so
many years…

9 789357 442022